LAND OF THE FREE
HOME OF THE BRAVE

For Priya, my lifeline.

PRELUDE

A SELF PUBLISHED BOOK

America is a mistake, a giant mistake
Attributed to Dr. Sigmund Freud

I am not a journalist, sociologist or political activist. I am not a history professor, scientist or philosopher. I am not an opinion leader or a psychiatrist. I know so little that I cannot say anything as complex as Dr. Freud allegedly said – that America is a giant mistake. Everyone knows that is untrue, so the doctor must have been playing with the machinations of our subconscious minds. Clever man.

Now that I have told you what I am not, let me tell you what I think I am. I am a Joe Blow. Everything I see or experience is in three categories – fun, funner and funnest. I work hard for a living (fun); I enjoy movies (funner). I am excited by the prospect of visiting the Statue of Liberty or Disneyland (funnest). On weekends, I buy groceries at a nearby mall. I like pizza. Hopefully, I am someone like you.

My research is shabby and always incomplete so if you are looking for academic precision you have the wrong book in your sight. In fact, whenever I wanted to check on something I looked up Wikipedia, a grand resource of information – in short, I have not gone too far beyond Wiki or the far reaches of my memory. So please do not take anything in this book as a guide or "reference" and have an argument with a friend about it. The chances are good that you will lose.

Why write? I really have no idea why I wrote this book. I realize saying that may not be cool. Being an introvert, I do not talk a lot so communicating with myself is a form of therapy. But as you may have figured out, speaking to oneself can raise suspicion. So writing helps – it is quiet, unobtrusive and soothing. Like on-line chess. I do that a lot.

Why publish? Again, I do not know. If having conversations with oneself is bad, imagine the perversion of allowing someone else to eavesdrop by publishing one's thoughts. Whatever the Freudian reason, I do not want to hear about it.

All that said, I do want to see the reaction I get. If it is horrendous you will see me watching even more TV than I do. If it is "reasonable" (as you can see I am not asking for much) I will publish a "conversation" I have been writing up for the past ten years. That stuff has an ominous name – it is called The Nine Dots and is almost like a séance where I have a LOT to say to one group of people who, in this recession, are probably wishing they were never born – young entrepreneurs.

Why publish on Amazon? A book as short as this will not be printed by anyone else. I know you like honesty.

Alexis de Tocqueville, a Frenchman, who wrote a book called the Discovery of America said, "In a revolution, as in a novel, the most difficult part to invent is the end." I have made it easy. There is no epilogue to the book. It just abruptly ends.

I have a couple of people to thank but you would not know them so I will spare you the Oscar speech. So there! I hope I have set your expectations properly. Enjoy the read.

Dilip Keshu

November 8, 2009, Princeton, New Jersey.

CHAPTER 1

LAND OF THE FREE

O! say can you see by the dawn's early light
What so proudly we hailed at the twilight's last gleaming.
Whose broad stripes and bright stars through the perilous
fight,
O'er the ramparts we watched were so gallantly streaming.
And the rockets' red glare, the bombs bursting in air,
Gave proof through the night that our flag was still there.
O! say does that star-spangled banner yet wave
O'er the land of the free and the home of the brave?
Stanza 1, the American National Anthem

The land of the free and the home of the brave is the United States of America, where I currently live. You may think the definition ("land of the free and the home of the brave") is a bit off, especially if you read popular rags, newspapers or watch TV. America is an intense place and that is how people feel when they live *inside* the country. If the abominations hurled on this great swath of land from people from nations, cities, towns, villages, streets, places of worship, schools and homes were like refuse and collected, the debris would fill the Milky Way.

The words, "the land of the free and the home of the brave" comes from the country's national anthem, a song that most American's struggle to sing (well) because its tune demands a vocal range of nearly two octaves. An amateur poet called Francis Scott Key penned four stanzas and titled his work, "Defence of Fort McHenry" after he witnessed British ships bombard a Baltimore fort of the same name (Fort McHenry) during the great American war of 1812. Soon after, this poem was set to the tune of a popular British drinking song (so no mystery here about the high requirements of vocal range that are needed to sing coherently). It was then renamed "The Star-Spangled Banner". On March 3rd, 1931 President Herbert Hoover affirmed the song as the national anthem.

The tune was not reworked. Roseanne Barr, a much loved comedienne was asked to sing the anthem at a 1990 San Diego Padres baseball game. It was so bad that it was not only booed and promptly called the "Great Screech" but joked about for a long time. She even made it to a TIME magazine list called the Top 10 National Anthem Renditions. Michael Bolton and R. Kelly, two accomplished singers also made that list. So if you screech it's okay.

When thirteen former British colonies declared independence from British rule in 1776, thereby creating a republic *for* the people, *of* the people and *by* the people, did anyone think it was really *free*? No.

That is what I think a colored female of that time would have said. A big NO.

The Nineteenth Amendment to the United States Constitution allowing women to vote was ratified only in 1920 and the Fifteenth Amendment which disallowed States to deny anyone the right to vote on the basis of "race, color, or previous condition of servitude" was ratified in 1870, some *94 years* after the Declaration of Independence. For years and years, state-sanctioned, racially-divisive "equal but separate laws" (often called Jim Crow laws) were in full force in many places in the country. It was not till around 1968, that most of these laws were undone. Even now, some who feel discriminated against will argue it is still not the land of the free. But *it is*. On a relative scale, no place is as free as this.

But do not be quick to judge Americans or remind them that they took so many years to right many wrongs or that young evolving countries will need time to get to where America is today. Americans want democracy everywhere. *Now*. These are a righteous people. They believe that no person is free until all people are free and as much as you tell them that the world has imperfections, they will be selectively deaf to your protestations. But look at the bright side – don't you want guys like that around?

Winston Churchill [1] once said, "A fanatic is one who cannot change his mind and will not change the subject". He was surely describing an American waxing eloquent on the concept of freedom.

So how do people feel about freedom in America today? Of course, it depends on the person you ask and in which country the question is posed. In more countries than you can name, you will be do well to plug your ears – because, you will hear a deafening roar of disgust and disapproval dominate silent nods of approval and soft affirmations. Now be prepared for a strange observation – you will need your earplugs in no country more than in the US itself!

But that's why Americans are "Americans". I know I have not defined them as a people yet but you will understand what I mean at some point in this short book. They can say what they like without fearing retribution from their government or suffer the tyranny

---

[1] Churchill was the wartime British Prime Minister and Nobel Laureate called Mahatma Gandhi, the father of modern India, a "fakir" whose when seen "striding half-naked up the steps of the viceregal palace" presented a sight that was "alarming and also nauseating". He certainly had a way with words.

of a lunatic leader. Everyone can have a view, however mad it is. No one needs to agree with another. *The ability to agree or disagree*, a freedom in itself, is absent in many "free" countries - it *is the single most important idea that defines freedom in America.*

The American constitution says, "All men are, by nature, *free* and independent, and have certain inalienable rights, among which are those of enjoying and defending life and *liberty*, acquiring, possessing, and protecting property, and seeking and obtaining happiness and safety." Freedom is an inalienable right.

Sometimes cultures do not know if they have inadvertently suppressed a small group into bondage of some kind. If they do it deliberately, it is because one right is considered more important than another and a compromise has to be made. We have to remind ourselves that the human race is *still evolving* culturally. This is why America, or any country for that matter, will never be absolutely and completely free. What was not acceptable in the past may be the norm today. What is not acceptable today is simply a problem waiting to be solved.

This country has scaled many barriers – some barely, some admirably – on gender, race, religion, politics, prostitution, drugs, euthanasia and abortion. It is still tackling the harder ones such as those pertaining to sexual preference. For example, should gays and lesbians be allowed to marry?

Many Americans will accept the union of same sex couples but not allow it to be called a marriage. There are some others who think such unions are illegal and unnatural. This is because words that define tradition and culture such as "marriage" take on different meanings when viewed from a cultural, social, economic, legal, biological or philosophical angle. In a diverse country such as America (a true melting pot) you can imagine how many views exist. And thus rages the great debate on these issues.

Remember the definition – "inalienable rights, among which are those of enjoying and defending life and liberty, acquiring, possessing, and protecting property, and *seeking and obtaining happiness* and safety". In theory, no one can stop a same sex couple from a union if that is what gives them happiness even if it violates religious laws. But sometimes the pursuit of happiness and safety cannot be at the cost of some other entity's rights. That's the puzzle this country and others will have to figure out. Over time solutions will be found, even if imperfect. I am the eternal optimist in the common sense of people.

Americans are slow to judge but quick to opine (if one would accept my distinction that a judgment is more permanent, an opinion more transient).

Only in American, can you say something really stupid and later recant the utterance saying you "misspoke". The country's greatest politicians say something daft and then apologize later – after all they misspoke. Such a gentle term, so disarming. Like misunderstand, misled. Unlike lied, exaggerated.

Senator Hillary Clinton, who I greatly admire, once said that she had to run with her head down to avoid sniper fire in Bosnia. She was immediately confronted with evidence that she had not been under any such threat and did not do what she so dramatically described. Her response was that she had misspoken.

On a TV show, Dick Cheney, former Vice President of the US, said he misspoke after accusing Saddam Hussein, the deposed ruler of Iraq, of possessing reconstituted nuclear weapons. We all know where that went - the allegation that Iraq's despot had weapons of mass destruction or WMDs propitiated the grounds for a full scale invasion.

Much loved American President Theodore Roosevelt, after whom teddy bears are named, wrote in his book, The Winning of the West, that "The world would have halted had it not been for the Teutonic conquests in alien lands; but the victories of Moslem over Christian have always proved a curse in the end. Nothing but sheer evil has come from the victories of Turk and Tartar." Sounds terrible, doesn't it?

But this is a man who eloquently wrote, "Practical equality of opportunity for all citizens, when we achieve it, will have two great results. *First*, every man will have a fair chance to make of himself all that in him lies; to reach the highest point to which his capacities, unassisted by special privilege of his own and unhampered by the special privilege of others, can carry him, and to get for himself and his family substantially what he has earned. *Second*, equality of opportunity means that the commonwealth will get from every citizen the highest service of which he is capable. No man who carries the burden of the special privileges of another can give to the commonwealth that service to which it is fairly entitled."

In 1912, he also spoke of women's rights at the National Convention of the Progressive Party. He said, "Working women have the same need to protection that working men have; the ballot is as necessary for one class as to the other; we do not believe that with the two sexes there is identity of function; but we do believe there should be equality of right." This was eight years before the Nineteenth Amendment was ratified.

Maybe Teddy Roosevelt "misspoke" about the Tartars and Turks. So, Teddy can be seen in two lights – one bad and one good. It is the same of all people and all countries. Nothing will change because human nature has a dark side. There will always be a dissenting view even if it is not manifest. Show me a saint and I will show you a flaw.

The bald eagle is a solitary bird. It does not hang around in flocks. It soars in the sky, with great majesty like the American spirit. It is a very apt that it is the national bird of this country. It is beautiful and strong. It does not do well under captivity and does not hunt in packs. It does not fly in formation with other birds. It does what it likes.

The US does the same – my sympathies to the United Nations and the Allies of this country. The big guy decides and the others have to come along. Oppose and you will see what a veto can do!

The charismatic British Prime Minister, Tony Blair (one of my favorites), was called George Bush's poodle for often having a consensus view with the US President. It is worse if a leader disagrees. When the French opposed the US invasion of Iraq in 2003, many American conservatives renamed the universally loved "French Fries" Freedom Fries. Even its cousin, the French Toast, was baptized and called Freedom Toast.

Only when they have to, and are united under a cause, do Americans fly in formation. When they do, it is a sight to behold - at war, at the Olympics; places where Team America has set out to win. Americans in these situations are bald eagles working as a team – strong, capable, focused and iron-willed.

If the eagle is synonymous with the people it represents, then the saying, "It takes a fool to feed himself to a bird of prey" takes on an ominous meaning for America's detractors. No country that has baited America has come off better and stronger. Those who think they have will realize in time that they made a mistake. Such is the power of this country. It is militarily, intellectually and economically the strongest country in the world.

Its strength comes from its freedom. Freedom is a state of mind more than it is a state of being. In America these ideas are conjoined. People are free and feel free. Everyone knows that freedom's child is success.

The national anthem of the People's Republic of China is called the March of the Volunteers. It goes somewhat like this:

> Arise, ye who refuse to be slaves!
> Let us amount our flesh and blood towards our new Great Wall!
> The Chinese nation faces its greatest peril,
> The thundering roar of our peoples will be heard!
> Arise! Arise! Arise!
> We are many, but our hearts beat as one!
> Selflessly braving the enemy's gunfire, march on!
> Selflessly braving the enemy's gunfire, march on!
> March on! March on! on!

The opening line talks about people not being enslaved and all through we hear exhortations to fight for what is dearest to all human beings – freedom. You can see the similarities with the American song: "And the rockets' red glare, the bombs bursting in air" and the Chinese, "Selflessly braving the enemy's gunfire, march on".

The song was provisionally adopted as the anthem in 1949 and officially ratified in 1982 by the Chinese Government. This anthem must have been sung during the years of the Great Leap Forward (1958 to 1963), a 5 year economic development program launched by Chairman Mao Zedong. The Great Leap was quite a leap (into a crevasse) when millions are said to have died from famine (some say 20 million, others 70 million! so the numbers are downright scary).

"March on!" they sang. With millions dead, hundreds of colossal blunders and a civil rights history that prompts freedom activists to bay like wolves on a full moon night have not stopped China's progress. It is a superpower today. While Americans may not call the Chinese "free", China is a free country. And a billion people would agree. The fact that many may not agree is natural – consensus is "old fashioned" and a rarity when it comes to public opinion. As I have said freedom is a state of mind more than it is a state of being.

The French National Anthem is similar. It asks people to listen to the onslaught of soldiers bent on slaughtering their "sons and wives" and exhorts people to fight for Liberté, Liberté chérie (Liberty, cherished liberty). Here is the first stanza of the La Marseillaise:

> Arise, children of the Fatherland,
> The day of glory has arrived!
> Against us the tyranny's
> Bloodied banner is raised,
> Bloodied banner is raised,
> Do you hear in the countryside
> The roar of those ferocious soldiers?
> They come right here into your midst
> To slaughter your sons and wives!

Later the song says that "traitors and conspiring kings" want to enslave everyone.

Interestingly, while the Indian national anthem sings of the glory of God, the protector of country, the British national anthem asks God to protect its (gracious and noble) Queen. We will just have to tackle that one in a separate book!

The path to freedom is strewn with calamity, hardship, sacrifice and gore. The American people saw their share of misery on the road to freedom but it pales when compared to what some other large nations have seen. Why is this so?

Because Americans are a civil lot. Rivers of blood did not flow in their struggle for freedom (I am being relative here). When First Viscount Cyril Radcliffe drew a line in the sand and separated India and Pakistan in 1947, a million people died[2]. You know the Chinese number. Americans know their limits and

---

[2] At the stroke of midnight on Aug 14th 1947, one of the oldest countries in the world, India, was separated into 3 countries – West Pakistan, East Pakistan (now Bangladesh) and India. Strangely, Pakistan (a child born from unified India) came into itself at 11:30pm on Aug 14th because the country adopted a new standard time (30 minutes before Indian Standard Time) creating what I call the Paradox of Creation – the independent child was half an hour older than its parent (an admittedly smaller India).

define what is good, bad and marginal, all within boundaries that most sane people would accept. I do not think a mass Nazi-like movement is possible within the US. Its people will not stand for it. Young Germans today have grown up with an acute awareness of what happened during the two great world wars. They had nothing to do with those events but are very sensitive to the subject. Some remain confused about the situation. Are they to atone for what happened before they were born? Why? [3] For the most part, the confusion does not lie in what the Nazis did to the Jews or the citizens of countries they attacked, defeated and occupied. The confusion is around why no one stopped Hitler and his party. How do you explain that?

Thomas Jefferson said, "All tyranny needs to gain a foothold is for people of good conscience to remain silent." That is what happened in Germany - the Nazi party gave a demoralized country of Germans hope and self esteem - hope of a better future and the belief that they were superior to others – they even got to promote the idea that they were a superior race of Aryans. The backdrop was a crushing World War I defeat and harsh impositions on the German state. It

---

[3] The irony is that Hitler was born an Austrian, not even a German.

took one mad man, Adolf Hitler, and his cohorts to lead a country to a war in which they conquered almost every country within reach of their army - at least for a while. They overran France in just under two months. Imagine that! Unfortunately, this war would ultimately cost seventy million lives and cause bloodshed in every major country in the world.

Today, many Germans are recovering from the realization that while their parents and grandparents may not have directly contributed to the war effort or killed anyone, they did not do enough to stop Hitler. Is it possible to see the rise of a Nazi-like movement in the US? I doubt it.

Firstly, the country never allows itself to believe it is inferior even when it is down. Americans have immense self pride and will not believe they are a downtrodden lot. They are eagles. They fly high. One cannot make this country's citizens do something foolish (like attack another) to make it feel superior.

They are a self effacingly honest with themselves (not that you will agree if you read or watch popular media!). If you stand on a soap box in Central Park and tell a bunch of guys who have lost their homes that you can take them to Eldorado, they will follow you till you find them a home. But if you violently dispossess an innocent citizen of his or her home and say, "Okay, now this belongs to you Mr. Homeless", Mr. Homeless will probably decline, call 911 or worse, knock you out.

Secondly, the idea of bravery, as I have defined it in the last chapter of this book (bravery is not about fighting *to get* something but all about *giving up* something bigger) has permeated all over America. This idea precludes any possibility of creating a tyrant. American is the most powerful country in the world. It has the strength to be a bully. Countries would have to think many times before opposing the might of a nation as large and wealthy as America. In other words, America could run amok if it wanted to but it has not. Americans will be prepared to give *everything* up if they have to stop another, even one of their own, from getting something unfairly. It is admittedly an odd thought, but one that keeps this country honest.

So are Americans a beautiful lot with no faults?

We wish.

A lot has been written of the Ugly American? Egregious, wealthy brats who lack discipline. An ugly side surfaces when opportunism, fueled by monetary motivation, rears its head! But I see ugly people everywhere. Greed is universal. It is ambition on steroids.

And yes, it has nothing to do with being American.

CHAPTER 2

FROM MANY, ONE

"Give me your tired, your poor,
Your huddled masses yearning to breathe free,
The wretched refuse of your teeming shore.
Send these, the homeless, tempest-tossed to me,
I lift my lamp beside the golden door!"
Emma Lazarus

Most Americans think that Christopher Columbus "discovered" America. He didn't. He landed in the Bahamas, Cuba, Jamaica and several other places but never in what we now call the United States of America. He was actually looking for India and so when he landed on what he thought to be that country he called the people Indios and that led to the indigenous people of America to be named Indians.

In 1507 a German cartographer called Martin Waldseemuller named America after Amerigo Vespucci, an Italian voyager. It would have been nice if Martin had picked a nice Native American name but America has a nice sound to it so all is well!

The etymology of the names of several states – Iowa, Massachusetts, Kansas, Illinois, Minnesota, Nebraska, Missouri, Oklahoma, Arkansas - leads to Native American words.

No one "discovered" America. And if anyone did, it was the Native Americans. Historical accounts will tell us that when the Europeans came to America there were already close to a million Native Americans thriving in this vast land.

Most people think that due to the colonization of American soil by England most people here have English ancestry. They are wrong. In fact there are more Americans of German and Irish descent than the English. The Italians are the fourth largest European ethnic group in America even though the country is named after one of their own. There are many Chinese, Filipino, Indian and Hispanic Americans too.

America is a melting pot but served as a salad – it has people of all hues and backgrounds all blended in but each proudly displays individuality. I have seen people saris and kaftans in Manhattan converse in fluent English. Perhaps not with the famous American twang but make no mistake - they are true blue yanks. I have even met some Americans whose English is worse than what comes off a religious séance when people are speaking in tongues.

That is what is confusing about this place. It transcends borders but has its own. It is commonplace yet unique. You can be Muslim, with parents in Egypt, go to a mosque, do the *namaz* five times a day, speak Arabic and yet be part of the American Armed Forces ready to do battle in Iraq. You can meet a Chinese engineer who eats ethnic food at home, speaks to his parents in China in Mandarin but carries an American passport and watches baseball.

The motto of the country is *E Pluribus Unum* which is Latin for *From Many, One.* Nothing captures the quintessential American more accurately than that one beautiful statement.

Americans are not parochial in their interests. Everything interests them. *Curious people, these!* They are collectively interested in everything because they are individually from everywhere. If you are Sudanese American you may be interested in what happens in Sudan – and because of that other Americans are tuned in, even though they have no direct ties to that country.

There are as many Jews in the US as there are in the homeland of the Judaism, Israel. So why wouldn't the Jews in America be interested in Israel and what happens with Palestine?

In 1983 the American army joined Jamaica and invaded Grenada. The excuse: the country was building an airstrip with communist Cuban help. You may need a map to find where this small country is. It is about the half size of the second smallest nation in Asia, Singapore. The CIA website says it is a country with "no regular military forces". The poor country must have been in shock, being invaded and defeated without a fight. The invading army had real guns. The alleged enemy's stockpile of coconuts was probably no match.

They will protect their borders even if means violating someone else's.

If it helps, the United Nations called the invasion "a flagrant violation of international law". Not that they could officially censure the big guy – America has an all important veto which it uses or threatens to use when other countries are a nuisance.

The Americans believe that their border is at the far edges of the universe even though the world would very much like them to stay within the confines of their 3.8 million square miles of homeland. This is because an American is American just as he or she is Irish, German, English, Indian, Chinese, Filipino, Brazilian, Italian, Danish, French, Portuguese, Spanish,

Russian and just about every other single ethic group you can name. Remember, Americans are collectively interested in everything because they are individually from everywhere.

I was told when I was young to avoid all discussions on race, religion and politics. Since these three topics define America in a sense let us skim through these three "hot" subjects. Just skim.....

Let us start with race. Almost everyone thinks of this in terms black and white, literally. If one were to ask whatever happened to the Native Americans there would be raised eyebrows! They were around for thousands of years before the English "discovered" America. In 1924, the Synder Act, also known as the Indian Citizenship Act, granted citizenship to all Native Americans – they were welcomed to become citizens of the country that was already theirs. Till 1938 or so, several states did not allow them to vote. Their numbers have not grown and they are hardly seen or heard these days – at least in the media.

The blacks on the other hand have struggled for equal rights for sixty years. Some 7 million people in the US have mixed ancestry and that number is growing. Rosa Parks, the famous black civil rights icon, had an Irish/Scot great grandfather. She also had some Cherokee blood in her. Eldrick Woods, also known as Tiger Woods, is part African American, Chinese Dutch and Cherokee. Obama, the first black President of the US, is of mixed blood too. The black scholar Henry Louis Gates is said to have remarked that some 58% of African-Americans have some European ancestry. I sometimes think that only God and black people know what is black. Since we are discussing a sensitive topic, I hasten to add that I mean this in a good sense. Think about it – we all came from Africa. So at what point did we stop becoming black? If it was that point in time when the color of our skin turned a pale shade then do today's fair skinned African Americans stop being black? Sometimes only a race can define itself especially when interracial unions are on the rise.

Blacks are the largest racial minority but Hispanics (or Latinos) are the largest ethnic group in America. In fifty years, it is anyone's guess what America will look like. Another generation of Americans will be born from interracial marriages and a wave of immigration from various countries will throw up more hues in the great American salad/melting pot.

Race will still be a hot topic for many more years to come in the US but I predict that in the lifetime of my grandchildren people will have to find something else to fight over and about.

Now let us come to religion. You have it all in America. Christianity, Judaism, Hinduism, Islam and hundreds of other religions flourish. People have the right to believe in any faith they choose to follow. But Christianity, Judaism and Islam are the center stage of the press. One can understand why these three are on the minds of many people - some 80% of the population is Christian (roughly 63% of those are Protestants) while Islam and Judaism are the second largest religious groups, even if a distant second by a large margin (around 2% each of the population).

Cassius Marcellus Clay, a Baptist Christian, and one of the greatest boxers of all time, converted to Islam in 1975 and took the name Mohammed Ali. You would think that Islam would be popular with many African Americans (some 12% of the population of the US) who have links to Africa where Islam is a leading religion. Not so, it appears. Apart from high profile conversions by the likes of Ali and Mike Tyson (who also converted to Islam) the country has a very small population of Muslims. No one knows how many Muslims live in the US but it is probably around seven million. As is true in most parts of the world, people do not spend time understanding religions that they themselves do not follow. Islam, like most things that are little understood, is feared in many quarters.

Never mind that Islam, Judaism and Christianity have common roots.

Only widespread education through popular media can help change the situation. During the 2009 Presidential election campaign some Americans were confused about Obama's religion. Many feared he was Muslim. So what if he was!

To add to the existing diversity, people can create their own religions. Ron Hubbard did just that. He founded the religion of Scientology which asks its members to believe that they are Thetans or immortal beings who reincarnate in Venus when their human form expires.

If religion was a defined as a set of practices and beliefs followed by a group of people, Money, Happiness and Comfort would be very strong contenders for the most popular religions in the US.

Politics. The Republican Party or the Grand Old Party (GOP) was founded by people who wanted to fight slavery in 1854. That single idea should have many African Americans queuing up to register themselves as Republicans. That was indeed the situation in the early days of the creation of the GOP. Over time, the majority of the African American vote has become Democratic.

It is very difficult to describe what a political party stands for these days but the GOP's standing position can be considered right off center which means it believes in free market economics and is conservative in its views. Its older rival, the Democratic Party has more registered voters and its standing position can be considered left of center meaning it tends to espouse socialist and more liberal views. Frankly, it is difficult to draw very clear distinctions between the two parties because on many issues they are close to the center. Americans vote along party lines but can very quickly change their vote if the other party fields a charming candidate. Presidents Clinton and Obama, both great orators, pulled votes from the other side. As did Reagan and Lincoln. There is a huge swath of people who have no affiliation to either the Democratic or Republican Party. I am fiscally conservative but socially liberal so I am never sure what I would do if asked to vote.

Sometimes party affiliation plays no part! I am sure there are groups who just vote for the best looking or "coolest" person. Some say height plays a part. The $5 bill has Abraham Lincoln's picture on it. He was the tallest President (6 ft 4 inches).

The somewhat rare $2 bill has Thomas Jefferson's picture on it. He was a tall President (6 ft 2 ½ inches). The most commonly found $1 bill has George Washington and he was also tall (6 ft 2 inches). General Ulysses Grant, on the $50 bill, was not tall (5 ft 8 inches) but then he won a war!

Benjamin Franklin is on the $100 bill and Alexander Hamilton is on the $10 bill. Neither were Presidents

Contrary to the belief in some quarters, this nation does not have a two party system. There are many other parties (some active and some not) – the Constitution Party, Green Party, America's First Party, America's Independent Party, Party for Socialism and Liberation, Objectivist Party and even a Natural Law Party. The Objectivist Party's philosophies were based on Ayn Rand's Objectivism as beautifully described in her books, The Fountainhead and Atlas

Shrugged. I remember reading these books when I was a teenager and wondering if was okay to admire Howard Roark! The Natural Law Party (disbanded in 2004) based its philosophy in part on the beliefs of Maharishi Mahesh Yogi, who promoted the use of transcendental meditation to cure the world of some of its ills.

Finally, in the Land of The Free you can create a party and chase your ideals if you feel strongly enough on an issue. Loretta Nall created the United States Marijuana Party in 2002. In its website it says that they feel "it is time for the 15 million Americans who smoke marijuana on a regular basis to stop hiding their love for this plant and unite as one large body of voters to demand an end to the unconstitutional prohibition of marijuana and the drug war". They seek to remove all penalties for adults 18 and over who choose to consume cannabis in a responsible manner.

So if you have a cause you could be a party founder and leader. This is America!

One of the most famous icons of America is the Statue of Liberty. It was a gift from the government of France to commemorate America's 100 years of independence (1886).

The statue, designed by Frederic Bartholdi and made by Gustave Eiffel's company (the same person who designed the Eiffel Tower) had a beautiful poem by Emma Lazarus engraved on a bronze plaque added to the pedestal of the statue in 1903. The poem says:

> "Give me your tired, your poor,
> Your huddled masses yearning to breathe free,
> The wretched refuse of your teeming shore."

It implores the world to send its unwanted masses to America. It promises to welcome them. The "refuse" of nations has created the greatest power in the world. Of course, it would be foolish to suggest that only the unwanted, poor and downtrodden came to America as it was quite the opposite - but no country has legally received more persecuted people than this country. In the wake of the Holocaust, America opened its borders to persecuted Jews – Today America has as many Jews as Israel has! America accepts more refugees than all of the next nine countries in the top 10 who accept displaced people. The number of illegal immigrants in the country (whose vast borders are not as impervious as people think) is in excess of several millions.

The best brains in the world come to the US to study and many stay on. Often they stay because America is a home away from home - they can get all that they seek from their home country right here in the US – ethnic food, friends, riches.

This is a place where you can go as high (or low) as you chose to go. The basic tenet of its social and economic philosophy is capitalism. Losers call it greed. Winners call it America!

American capitalism forces meritocracy. If you are good there is no limit to what you can achieve. This is a nation of people who are relentless in the pursuit of a better life. Some will say it is a nation of people who are relentless in the pursuit of money. A better life is a by-product of money. M*oney* has *one* at its center – the priority many people give it in the busy lives they lead.

We must remember that Americans *give and take*. Americans give over $300 billion to charitable causes every year. No country comes close.

I must confess that at times I worry about the new generation. They are so difficult to please. Something has to be "over the top" to be admired. "Humungous" is a commonly used term with the young. I never used that word when I was growing up. It means extraordinarily large.

Old fashion movie stunts have been replaced by intense computer generated imagery or CGI action. Villains can't be cruel enough so they have started to take alien forms! Reading "literature quality" books is considered a nerdy pastime.

I have heard kids speak of a having had a "tough day". That means just going to school and back. Back in my time, a tough day meant something far more serious. Do not be surprised if you frequently hear "I am bored" and "I am tired" from a person who has not done much – in the first instance, he or she has not done much to change the situation and in the second, done anything at all!

That said, the new generation is not to be underestimated. They are stronger and brighter than us. Unfortunately we will know how this blessed lot will fare only when tested by an experience none of us would like to face in our lifetime.

We hardly know ourselves even after a lifetime of "discovery". It is best not to try and define an American and if you do stick to some generalities – they are a generous, intelligent, hard working, brave lot who make their share of mistakes and are as human as all of us.

Let us wrap this up and move to the final chapter of this book.

CHAPTER 3

HOME OF THE BRAVE

And where is that band who so vauntingly swore
That the havoc of war and the battle's confusion,
A home and a country should leave us no more!
Their blood has washed out their foul footsteps' pollution.
No refuge could save the hireling and slave
From the terror of flight, or the gloom of the grave:
And the star-spangled banner in triumph doth wave
O'er the land of the free and the home of the brave.

Stanza 3, the American National Anthem

Everyone I have met seems to know where he or she was when the terrorists flew their planes into the World Trade Center. 9/11[4] is etched in our personal memories and collective history because on that day in 2001 the world bore witness to the destructive

---

[4]   9/11 is 11th September and not 9th November (the day that commemorates the Fall of the Berlin Wall) thanks again to the Americans being unique. The unique date format used by the Americans has a very small following: Belize, Canada, the Philippines and Pulau and the Federated States of Micronesia. But we know what Americans are – eagles. They fly majestically to their own design.

power of the darkest, cruelest side of human beings. We remember 9/11, not because of the loss of life - there are surely many regional conflicts, acts of genocide in barbaric places and natural calamities that have caused greater loss of life – but because of the thousands of acts of courage, sacrifice and heroism demonstrated on that day and after, which have altered the course of our lives and the history of nations. Most records say that on that day 2,974 innocent people died. Actually, 2,993 people died. 19 of them were hijackers. They were people too even if misguided, cruel ones.

What hijacker Mohamed Atta and his fellow conspirators did is something unimaginable by most of us - sacrificing one's life for a cause. Most people overtly condemn the attacks even while contemplating the numbing audacity of the plan of the hijackers. It is one thing to have a single person sacrifice his life for a cause. To do this with no fewer than 19 others *and* not being caught is quite another. Not counting random suicide bombers, the last time we saw such organized attacks where one life was traded for several was in Oct 1944 - the Kamikaze of World War II. Kamikaze translates to "divine wind". What one party thought of as being divine (the ultimate sacrifice) the other thought of being the opposite – satanic, stupid, irrational and desperate.

Everyone will agree that Atta's act was cruel. But was it brave or cowardly? Yes to both - it depends on whom you ask. That's how strange our world is.

Bravery is a highly coveted quality in human beings. This is what it means to me - bravery is almost never about fighting to *get* or keep something you treasure but all about *giving up* or being prepared to give up something bigger. If you are fighting for freedom (a huge idea) and are prepared to give up your life (much bigger than "freedom"), that is bravery. In that context, there is no country as brave as America.

It will poke its nose in hot spots if it has to do "the right thing". It will send its armed forces into horrendous situations where it knows the loss of life will be in several thousands if it believes it is doing the right thing. Remember Vietnam where American lost 58,000 soldiers? What were the Americans doing there anyway?

The French, who had Vietnam under control for several years, lost control to Japan during World War II only to regain notional control after the war. The Viet Minh force assembled by Nguyen Ai Quoc (later known as Ho Chi Minh) to fight the French was supported by Communist China. After fighting a losing war, the French decided to leave Vietnam and several factions (let us just say a northern one backed by Communists and a southern one backed by the US) clamored for power.

In 1954 the Geneva Accords separated the countries along the 17th parallel with the hope that the north and south would unite after a referendum. Needless to say that did not work and a war between the north and south broke out. The US which believed if one country fell to the Communists others would fall in succession (Domino Theory) stepped in not just with financial aid but direct military assistance. It is estimated that 2.5 million American soldiers fought in Vietnam. That is a staggering number considering that the conflict was miles away from home.

The Vietnam War was a brave one even if costly in terms of life and suffering. Even if the immediate outcome was not a successful one. American intervention was brave because Americans were willing to give up their lives for something they believed was fundamentally wrong – the spread of communism.

So were the Americans who opposed the war cowards? No. At some stage, the American public was willing to give up their honor of being the best armed force in the world and admit defeat in a small country. Withdrawing from a posture is also bravery – being prepared to give up a "thing" for something bigger. Too often we fail to give up. We take a posture that is not good and all of our subsequent actions are aimed to fortify our stance even though deep down we *know* we are not in a good position. Things only get worse over time unless luck intervenes. At some stage we pass the point of no return. Often, we have seen this happen in financial scandals. One mistake, one cover up and then a series of actions take the unfortunate party past the point of no return.

We all know how the story of communism ended. Sometimes we lose a battle to win a war. And thus, The Land of the Free and the Home of the Brave, endures.

Thanks for reading and staying with me so far into the book. I warned you that this book would have no epilogue and that it would end abruptly.

Like this.

www.ingramcontent.com/pod-product-compliance
Lightning Source LLC
Chambersburg PA
CBHW071256280526
45788CB00004B/1737